The Book Of DINOSAURS
AND
PREHISTORIC LIFE

Dear Parents:

This book is designed as an introduction to dinosaurs. We recommend that you learn about these ancient animals along with your children.

Our knowledge of dinosaurs is based upon skeletal remains and fossils discovered all over the world. Much of what we know is derived from scientific evidence but some knowledge is based on speculation of what scientists believe to be true.

Dinosaurs died out suddenly 65 million years ago. No one is certain as to why this happened.

As new and exciting discoveries are made, we will gain a better understanding of our past and the animals that roamed the earth millions of years ago. New theories and information will alter our opinions as scientists strive to unlock the mystery of the dinosaurs.

MJ STUDIOS INC.
Michael Denman
William Huiett

WRITTEN BY
Carol Z. Bloch

ACANTHOPHOLIS
(AH-KAN-THOF-O-LISS)
"THORNBEARER"

INTERESTING FACTS:

The **Acanthopholis** was a plant-eating animal that was one of the smaller dinosaurs. Its back legs were longer than its front legs. Small armored plates covered its heavy body. Spikes stuck out from its neck and shoulders.

When It Lived

LATE CRETACEOUS

Size

17 FEET

Weight

2 TONS (4,000 POUNDS)

ALBERTOSAURUS
(AL-BER-TUH-SAWR-US)
"ALBERTA LIZARD"

WHERE IT WAS FOUND

NORTH AMERICA

INTERESTING FACTS:

The **Albertosaurus** was a dangerous giant meat eater. With ferocious teeth in its huge head, it was able to kill its prey very quickly. This creature walked on its thick hind legs and had little use of its short front legs. Scientists have discovered many skeletons of this dinosaur in the United States.

When It Lived

LATE CRETACEOUS

Size

26 FEET

Weight

2 TONS (4,000 POUNDS)

ALLOSAURUS
(AL-UH-SAWR-US)
"DIFFERENT LIZARD"

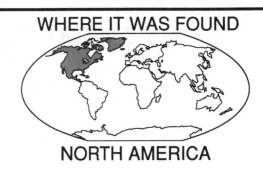
INTERESTING FACTS:

The **Allosaurus** was a huge dinosaur with a tremendous head and a long, powerful tail. This meat eater's head had an unusual bony ridge that ran from its eyes to its snout. It had sharp teeth and could swallow its prey whole. Remains have been found all over the world.

When It Lived

LATE JURASSIC

Size

36 FEET

Weight

**1-2 TONS
(2,000-4,000 POUNDS)**

ALTISPINAX
(AL-TUH-SPY-NAX)
"HIGH SPINES"

When It Lived

EARLY CRETACEOUS

Size

26 FEET

Weight

3 TONS (6,000 POUNDS)

INTERESTING FACTS:

The **Altispinax** had a sail-like fan across its back. This fan was held together with very large spines and may have helped cool the animal down in hot weather. Sets of very small teeth enabled it to chew meat easily.

ANATOSAURUS
(AH-NAT-UH-SAWR-US)
"DUCK LIZARD"

WHERE IT WAS FOUND

NORTH AMERICA

When It Lived

LATE CRETACEOUS

INTERESTING FACTS:

The **Anatosaurus** was one of the last dinosaurs to become extinct. It was a plant eater with 1,000 small teeth in its horny bill. Strong back legs enabled it to run very fast to escape its enemies. Several skin impressions found show the skin was rough and bumpy.

Size

30 FEET

Weight

3 TONS (6,000 POUNDS)

ANCHICERATOPS
(AN-KEE-SER-A-TOPS)
"NEAR-HORNED FACE"

WHERE IT WAS FOUND

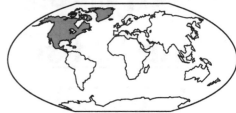

NORTH AMERICA

INTERESTING FACTS:

The plant-eating **Anchiceratops** had a small horn on its nose and two long horns above its eyes. A large, bony frill grew from its neck to its shoulders. This frill was different than those on other frilled dinosaurs which may have helped these animals recognize each other.

When It Lived

LATE CRETACEOUS

Size

19 FEET

Weight

7 TONS (14,000 POUNDS)

ANCHISAURUS
(ANG-KEE-SAWR-US)

"NEAR LIZARD"

NORTH AMERICA,
AFRICA AND EUROPE

Size

6 FEET

Weight

60 POUNDS

When It Lived

LATE TRIASSIC/EARLY JURASSIC

INTERESTING FACTS:

The **Anchisaurus** was one of the first
dinosaurs on earth. It was small and moved quickly
on all fours. It had large strong claws on each thumb
that it probably used to help it eat both plants and
animals. Fossils found show that it lived in many
parts of the world.

ANKYLOSAURUS
(ANG-KILE-UH-SAWR-US)

"STIFFENED LIZARD"

WHERE IT WAS FOUND

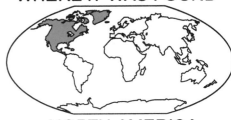

NORTH AMERICA

INTERESTING FACTS:

The **Ankylosaurus** was covered with armored plates. These bumpy plates
on its body, head and tail protected it from its enemies. A large club at the end
of its tail probably helped it ward off flesh eaters. Although it looked fierce,
it was very peaceful and spent
much of its time looking
for plants to eat.

When It Lived

LATE CRETACEOUS

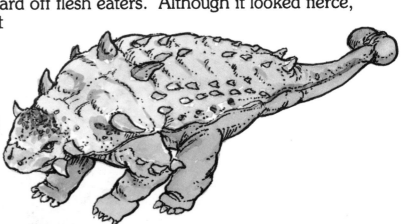

Size

35 FEET

Weight

5 TONS (10,000 POUNDS)

APATOSAURUS
(AH-PAT-UH-SAWR-US)
"DECEPTIVE LIZARD"

INTERESTING FACTS:

The **Apatosaurus** was a giant dinosaur that used to be known as Brontosaurus. The combination of a heavy body, thick legs and a very long neck and tail made it a very slow moving animal. Its brain was small compared to the rest of its body.

This four-legged plant eater had to consume a tremendous amount of food to satisfy its enormous appetite. It may have spent much of its time in water but was also able to support its weight on land. Small peg-shaped teeth enabled it to chew its food.

When It Lived

LATE JURASSIC

Size

75 FEET

Weight

**33 TONS
(66,000 POUNDS)**

ARCHAEOPTERYX
(AR-KEE-OP-TER-IX)
"ANCIENT WING"

WHERE IT WAS FOUND

EUROPE

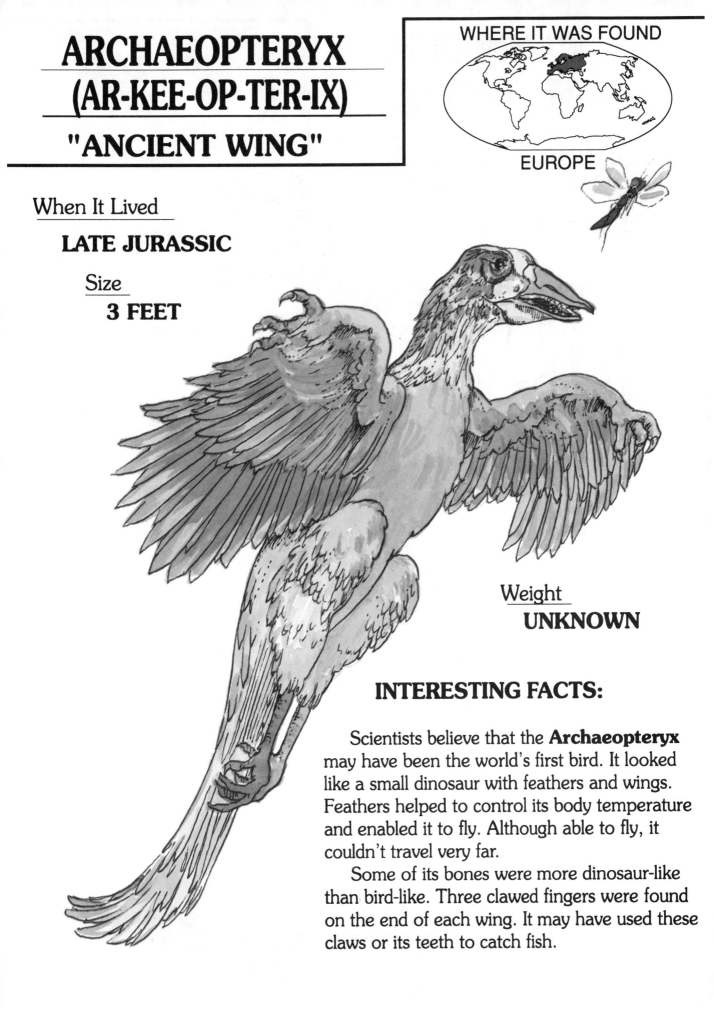

When It Lived

LATE JURASSIC

Size

3 FEET

Weight

UNKNOWN

INTERESTING FACTS:

Scientists believe that the **Archaeopteryx** may have been the world's first bird. It looked like a small dinosaur with feathers and wings. Feathers helped to control its body temperature and enabled it to fly. Although able to fly, it couldn't travel very far.

Some of its bones were more dinosaur-like than bird-like. Three clawed fingers were found on the end of each wing. It may have used these claws or its teeth to catch fish.

AVIMIMUS
(A-VEE-MY-MUS)
"BIRD MIMIC"

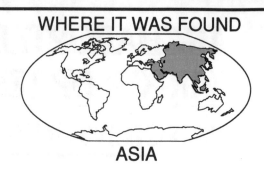

ASIA

When It Lived

LATE CRETACEOUS

Size

3-5 FEET

Weight

25 POUNDS

INTERESTING FACTS:

The **Avimimus** was nicknamed "Bird Mimic" because it so resembled a bird. Although it had wings, it may not have been able to fly. Long bird-like feet enabled it to run very fast after lizards and insects.

BACTROSAURUS
(BACK-TRUH-SAWR-US)
"STAFF LIZARD"

INTERESTING FACTS:

The **Bactrosaurus** was a duck-billed dinosaur that liked to eat plants and shrubs. It could store food in its cheeks for later use. Scientists are not sure what the top of its head looked like because no skull was ever found.

WHERE IT WAS FOUND

ASIA

When It Lived

MIDDLE CRETACEOUS

Size

13-20 FEET

Weight

**1-2 TONS
(2,000-4,000 POUNDS)**

BAGACERATOPS
(BAH-GAH-SAIR-UH-TOPS)
"SMALL HORNED FACE"

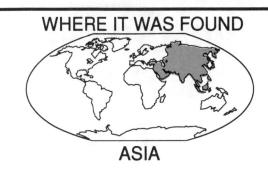

ASIA

INTERESTING FACTS:

The **Bagaceratops** was a four-legged plant eater. This small dinosaur had a parrot-like beak that helped it tear up plants to eat. It had one small horn above its beak and a small frill protected its neck.

When It Lived

LATE CRETACEOUS

Size

3 FEET

Weight

1,000 POUNDS

BRACHIOSAURUS
(BROCK-EE-O-SAWR-US)
"ARM LIZARD"

WHERE IT WAS FOUND

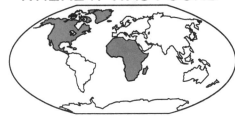

NORTH AMERICA AND AFRICA

INTERESTING FACTS:

The **Brachiosaurus** was one of the largest dinosaurs to roam the earth. Its thick front legs were longer than its back legs. It probably lived in herds in the wooded plains and ate leaves from treetops. It may have had two brains, one in its head and the other in its tail.

When It Lived

LATE JURASSIC

Weight

75 TONS (150,000 POUNDS)

Size

74 FEET LONG
39 FEET HIGH

BRACHYCERATOPS
(BRAK-EE-SAIR-UH-TOPS)
"SHORT HORNED FACE"

INTERESTING FACTS:

The **Brachyceratops** was one of the smallest of the horned dinosaurs. Only five fossils of this dinosaur have ever been found. They were found together all in one place. Although few have been discovered, we know it had a large horn on its nose, two horns over its eyebrows and a short neck frill.

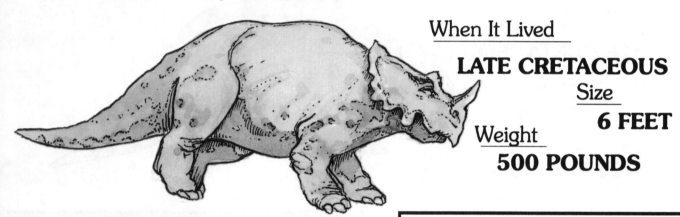

When It Lived

LATE CRETACEOUS

Size

6 FEET

Weight

500 POUNDS

CAMARASAURUS
(KAM-UH-RUH-SAWR-US)
"CHAMBERED LIZARD"

WHERE IT WAS FOUND

NORTH AMERICA

INTERESTING FACTS:

The brain of the **Camarasaurus** was very small compared to its huge body. Its front legs were nearly as long as its hind legs. Flesh eaters probably left it alone because of its tough skin and large size. It continually ate leaves and plants it found growing close to the ground.

When It Lived

LATE JURASSIC

Size

60 FEET

Weight

20 TONS (40,000 POUNDS)

CAMPTOSAURUS
(KAMP-TUH-SAWR-US)
"BENT LIZARD"

When It Lived

**LATE JURASSIC/
EARLY CRETACEOUS**

Size

4-23 FEET

Weight

UP TO 1,100 POUNDS

INTERESTING FACTS:

The **Camptosaurus** had hooved feet that helped it quickly escape from an enemy. Although it was bent over, it could stand up straight and use its long tongue to gather leaves. It had a spike-shaped thumb on each hand.

CARNOTAURUS
(KAR-NO-TAWR-US)
"MEAT-EATING BULL"

WHERE IT WAS FOUND

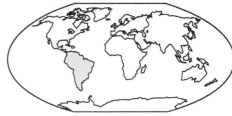

SOUTH AMERICA

When It Lived

LATE CRETACEOUS

Size

40 FEET

Weight

UNKNOWN

INTERESTING FACTS:

The **Carnotaurus** was a vicious meat-eating dinosaur. It had a short snout with two large horns over its eyes. Its skin was rough and pebbly which was unusual for a meat eater.

CENTROSAURUS
(SEN-TRUH-SAWR-US)
"SHARP POINT LIZARD"

WHERE IT WAS FOUND

NORTH AMERICA

INTERESTING FACTS:

The **Centrosaurus** had an unusual horn on its nose that bent forward instead of back. Its bumpy frill had two long, hook-like bones projecting from the top of its head. This plant-eating dinosaur may have traveled in herds.

When It Lived
LATE CRETACEOUS

Size
20 FEET

Weight
2 TONS (4,000 POUNDS)

CERATOSAURUS
(SAIR-AT-O-SAWR-US)
"HORNED LIZARD"

WHERE IT WAS FOUND

NORTH AMERICA

INTERESTING FACTS:

The **Ceratosaurus** was a fierce meat eater with very sharp teeth. It had an unusual blade-like horn on its nose and small, bony plates down the middle of its back. This savage hunter probably stalked its prey in packs.

When It Lived
LATE JURASSIC

Size
20 FEET

Weight
1 TONS (2,000 POUNDS)

CETIOSAURUS
(SEET-EE-O-SAWR-US)
"WHALE LIZARD"

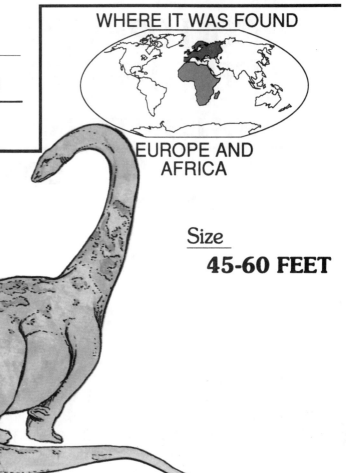

EUROPE AND AFRICA

INTERESTING FACTS:

The **Cetiosaurus** was a giant plant-eating dinosaur. It had a long neck, blunt head and spoon-shaped teeth. When its skeleton was first found, scientists thought it may have been a whale.

Size

45-60 FEET

When It Lived

MIDDLE TO LATE JURASSIC

Weight

**9-12 TONS
(18,000-24,000 POUNDS)**

CHASMOSAURUS
(KAZ-MUH-SAWR-US)
"OPENING LIZARD"

WHERE IT WAS FOUND

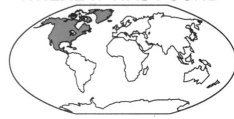

NORTH AMERICA

INTERESTING FACTS:

The **Chasmosaurus** was a plant-eating dinosaur with a small horn on its nose and one above each eye. It had a large bony neck frill covered with skin. Holes in this frill made it lighter in weight. Scales all over its body protected it from predators.

Size

17 FEET

When It Lived

LATE CRETACEOUS

Weight

**3-5 TONS
(6,000-10,000 POUNDS)**

COELOPHYSIS
(SEE-LO-FISE-ISS)
"HOLLOW FORM"

NORTH AMERICA

When It Lived
LATE TRIASSIC

Size
3 FEET

Weight
100 POUNDS

INTERESTING FACTS:

The **Coelophysis** was one of the first dinosaurs on earth. It was a very fast-running dinosaur. The Coelophysis looked very much like a lizard with a long, snaky neck and was the size of a large dog. It ran on its back legs and used the sharp claws on each hand to catch small animals.

COELURUS
(SEE-LURE-US)
"HOLLOW BONES"

WHERE IT WAS FOUND

NORTH AMERICA

INTERESTING FACTS:

The **Coelurus** was a small lightweight dinosaur. It had three fingers on each hand with small claws on two of the fingers. These claws helped it catch tiny animals and birds. It may also have eaten dinosaur eggs and berries.

When It Lived
LATE JURASSIC

Size
**6 FEET LONG,
3 FEET TALL**

Weight
30 POUNDS

COMPSOGNATHUS
(KOMP-SO-NAY-THUS)
"ELEGANT JAW"

Size
2 FEET

Weight
7 POUNDS

When It Lived
LATE JURASSIC

INTERESTING FACTS:

The **Compsognathus** was one of the smallest dinosaurs on earth. It was about the size of a chicken and had a tail longer than its head and body. This stiff tail enabled it to keep its balance. It ran very swiftly on its two hind bird-like legs.

Though small in size, it was a good predator. Sharp teeth and two-fingered hands helped it catch and hold its prey. Insects and small reptiles were its primary food. We know much about what it ate because the skeleton of a small lizard was found within its skeletal remains.

CORYTHOSAURUS
(KO-RITH-UH-SAWR-US)
"HELMET LIZARD"

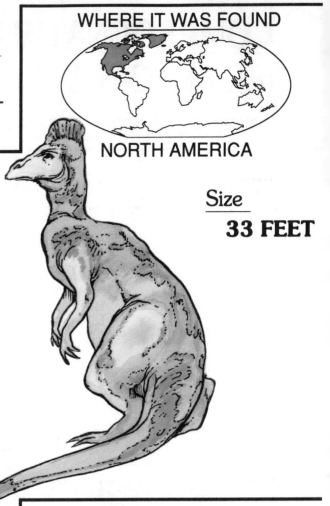

NORTH AMERICA

When It Lived

LATE CRETACEOUS

Size

33 FEET

Weight

**2-4 TONS
(4,000-8,000 POUNDS)**

INTERESTING FACTS:

The **Corythosaurus** had a very large helmet-shaped crest on the top of its head. This unusual crest was narrow and hollow. It used its large tail for balance when it stood on its back legs. This fast runner probably ate insects and plants.

DACENTRURUS
(DAY-SEN-TROO-RUS)
"VERY SPINY LIZARD"

WHERE IT WAS FOUND

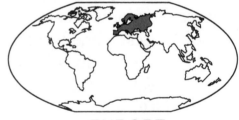

EUROPE

INTERESTING FACTS:

The **Dacentrurus** had two rows of huge spikes going down its back and tail. These spikes were its only means of protection. It used its spiked tail to ward off its enemies. A small head and little teeth allowed it to feed on soft plants.

Weight
1,500 POUNDS

Size
13 FEET

When It Lived

**MIDDLE TO
LATE JURASSIC**

DASPLETOSAURUS
(DASS-PLEE-TUH-SAWR-US)
"FRIGHTFUL LIZARD"

NORTH AMERICA

Size

28 FEET

When It Lived

LATE CRETACEOUS

Weight

4 TONS (8,000 POUNDS)

INTERESTING FACTS:

The **Daspletosaurus** was a relative of the Tyrannosaurus but was smaller and faster. It had a powerful head with huge jaws and lots of sharp teeth. Its front arms were small and weak and each had only two fingers. This savage hunter attacked and ate other dinosaurs.

DEINONYCHUS
(DINE-O-NYE-KUS)
"TERRIBLE CLAW AND OPPOSING HANDS"

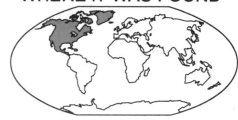

NORTH AMERICA

Size

11 FEET LONG
5 FEET HIGH

Weight

170 POUNDS

When It Lived

EARLY CRETACEOUS

INTERESTING FACTS:

The **Deinonychus** was a very powerful meat eater that would hunt in packs for animals even larger than itself. It used its very long tail for balance while it used its huge claws and feet to kill its prey. Each foot had a sharp claw that could go in and out whenever it was needed. Although it was a small dinosaur, it had a large brain and was a quick and clever hunter.

DILOPHOSAURUS
(DYE-LO-FUH-SAWR-US)
"TWO-CRESTED LIZARD"

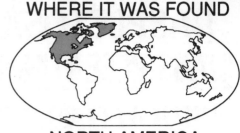
INTERESTING FACTS:

The **Dilophosaurus** had two bony crests running along the top of its nose to the back of its head. This ferocious meat eater had powerful legs and was fast on its feet. Enemies tried to escape the sharp claws on its fingers and toes.

When It Lived

EARLY JURASSIC

Size

20 FEET

Weight

1,500 POUNDS

DIMETRODON
(DYE-MET-RUH-DON)
"TWO-MEASURE TEETH"

WHERE IT WAS FOUND

NORTH AMERICA

INTERESTING FACTS:

The **Dimetrodon** lived before dinosaurs roamed the earth. This lizard-like reptile had a large sail along its back. This sail probably helped control its body temperature. It is the largest known meat eater of the pre-dinosaur period.

When It Lived

PERMIAN

Weight

UNKNOWN

Size

11 FEET

DIMORPHODON
(DYE-MORF-UH-DON)
"TWO-SHAPE TEETH"

EUROPE

INTERESTING FACTS:

The **Dimorphodon** was one of the earliest flying reptiles. It had an enormous head and long tail. On each hand it had one long finger that helped support each wing. Fish and other small creatures may have been its main diet.

Weight
UNKNOWN

Size
3 FEET

When It Lived

EARLY TO LATE JURASSIC

DIPLODOCUS
(DIH-PLOD-UH KUS)
"DOUBLE BEAM"

WHERE IT WAS FOUND

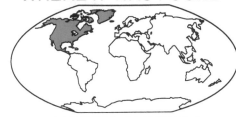

NORTH AMERICA

When It Lived
LATE JURASSIC

Size
87 FEET

INTERESTING FACTS:

The **Diplodocus** was one of the longest dinosaurs that ever lived. Its long, snaky neck allowed it to graze on the top of trees. It could whip its long tail back and forth to scare off attackers. Hooked claws helped protect it against other dinosaurs. Two rows of small peg-like teeth were used to chew leaves.

Weight
7-11 TONS
(14,000-22,000 POUNDS)

DROMAEOSAURUS
(DROM-EE-UH-SAWR-US)
"SWIFT LIZARD"

When It Lived

LATE CRETACEOUS

Size

6 FEET

Weight
100 POUNDS

INTERESTING FACTS:

The **Dromaeosaurus** was about the size of man. While running it used its stiff tail to help keep its balance. This vicious dinosaur was a great hunter. Each foot had a knife-like toe it used to attack small animals.

DROMICEIOMIMUS
(DRO-MISS-EE-O-MY-MUS)
"EMU MIMIC"

WHERE IT WAS FOUND

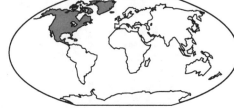

NORTH AMERICA

INTERESTING FACTS:

The **Dromiceiomimus** looked like an ostrich with a long tail and no feathers. This intelligent animal may have been the fastest of all dinosaurs. It was easy prey unless it was able to run quickly from its enemies. Because it had no teeth, it probably ate plants, seeds and insects.

When It Lived

LATE CRETACEOUS

Size

11 FEET

Weight
220 POUNDS

DRYOSAURUS
(DRY-O-SAWR-US)
"OAK LIZARD"

EUROPE AND
NORTH AMERICA

Weight
170 POUNDS

When It Lived

MIDDLE/LATE JURASSIC

Size

12 FEET

INTERESTING FACTS:

The **Dryosaurus** was a small, fast-running animal that ran and walked on the toes of its hind legs. While it watched carefully for predators, its stiff tail helped it keep its balance. Plants made up most of its diet.

EDMONTOSAURUS
(ED-MON-TUH-SAWR-US)
"EDMONTON LIZARD"

WHERE IT WAS FOUND

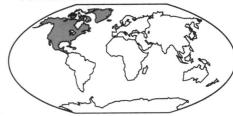

NORTH AMERICA

INTERESTING FACTS:

The **Edmontosaurus** was a large duck-billed dinosaur with a spoon-shaped beak. It walked on its hind legs and chewed tree leaves and pine needles with its hundreds of teeth. Some believe it had loose skin on the side of its nose that it blew up like a balloon to help it make a loud noise.

When It Lived

LATE CRETACEOUS

Size

33 FEET

Weight
3 TONS (6,000 POUNDS)

ELAPHROSAURUS
(EH-LOFF-RUH-SAWR-US)
"LIGHTWEIGHT LIZARD"

When It Lived
LATE JURASSIC

Size
11 FEET

Weight
220 POUNDS

INTERESTING FACTS:

The **Elaphrosaurus** was one of the earliest ostrich-like dinosaurs. It was an intelligent animal with keen eyesight. Thin legs enabled it to run quickly from danger. Since it had no teeth, it probably ate plants and insects.

EOCERATOPS
(EE-O-SAIR-UH-TOPS)
"DAWN HORNED FACE"

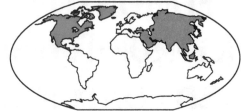
INTERESTING FACTS:

The **Eoceratops** had a three foot long skull with three small horns. A horn on its nose curved slightly forward and a horn over each eye curved toward its back. This plant-eating dinosaur had a short bony neck frill that helped protect it.

When It Lived
LATE CRETACEOUS

Size
20 FEET

Weight
**2-5 TONS
(4,000-10,000 POUNDS)**

ERLIKOSAURUS
(ER-LIK-UH-SAWR-US)

"ERLIK'S LIZARD"

Weight
280 POUNDS

Size
13 FEET

When It Lived
LATE CRETACEOUS

INTERESTING FACTS:

The **Erlikosaurus** is different than any other dinosaur known to man. An unusual skull with a very long, thin toothless beak made it unique. Sharp pointed teeth lined the sides of its jaw. It had very large clawed feet that may have been webbed.

EUOPLOCEPHALUS
(YOU-OP-LUH-SEF-UH-LUS)

"WELL-ARMED HEAD"

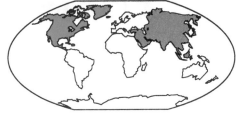
INTERESTING FACTS:

The **Euoplocephalus** was a well-armored dinosaur with sheets of bone and rows of spines down its back. It had a heavy bony club at the end of its tail it used to protect itself. This plant eater had a horny, toothless beak.

When It Lived
LATE CRETACEOUS

Size
23 FEET

Weight
3 TONS (6,000 POUNDS)

FABROSAURUS
(FAB-RUH-SAWR-US)
"FABRE'S LIZARD"

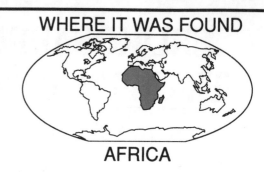

AFRICA

INTERESTING FACTS:

The **Fabrosaurus** was an early dinosaur that was smaller than man. Its hind legs were very strong which enabled it to run very fast from nearby enemies. Rows of strong, ridged teeth lined its jaws, so it could grind roots and other vegetation.

When It Lived

LATE TRIASSIC/EARLY JURASSIC

Size
3 FEET

Weight
40 POUNDS

GERANOSAURUS
(JER-AN-O-SAWR-US)
"CRANE LIZARD"

WHERE IT WAS FOUND

AFRICA

INTERESTING FACTS:

The **Geranosaurus** was a small dinosaur with a very unusual feature. It had more than one kind of tooth in its head. This plant eater had teeth for cutting and grinding, and tusks in its jaw. It had long, slender legs and was lightly built.

When It Lived

LATE TRIASSIC/EARLY JURASSIC

Size
4 FEET Weight
50 POUNDS

HADROSAURUS
(HAD-RO-SAWR-US)
"BIG LIZARD"

NORTH AMERICA

When It Lived
LATE CRETACEOUS

Weight
3 TONS
(6,000 POUNDS)

Size
26-32 FEET

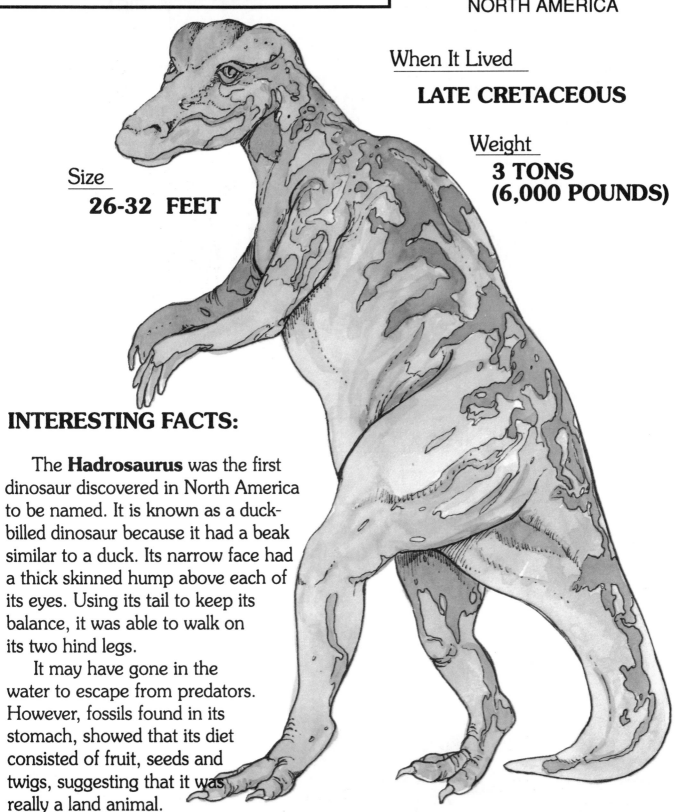

INTERESTING FACTS:

The **Hadrosaurus** was the first dinosaur discovered in North America to be named. It is known as a duck-billed dinosaur because it had a beak similar to a duck. Its narrow face had a thick skinned hump above each of its eyes. Using its tail to keep its balance, it was able to walk on its two hind legs.

It may have gone in the water to escape from predators. However, fossils found in its stomach, showed that its diet consisted of fruit, seeds and twigs, suggesting that it was really a land animal.

HETERODONTOSAURUS
(HET-ER-UH-DON-TUH-SAWR-US)
"DIFFERENT-TOOTHED LIZARD"

AFRICA

When It Lived

**LATE TRIASSIC/
EARLY JURASSIC**

INTERESTING FACTS:

The **Heterodontosaurus** had three different types of teeth. It used its front teeth for cutting, molars for grinding, and had fangs on its lower jaw. Each foot had a claw at the back of its heel. This plant-eating dinosaur was able to run quickly to escape its enemies.

Size
4 FEET

Weight
50 POUNDS

HOMALOCEPHALE
(HO-MAH-LUH-SEF-UH-LEE)
"EVEN HEAD"

WHERE IT WAS FOUND

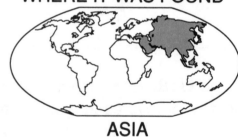

ASIA

INTERESTING FACTS:

The **Homalocephale** had a very thick skull with several bumps on the top of its head. It walked on its back legs and used its tail to help keep its balance. This dinosaur may have been about the size of a very large goat and ate mostly plants.

When It Lived

LATE CRETACEOUS

Size
10 FEET

Weight
200 POUNDS

HYLAEOSAURUS
(HY-LAY-EE-UH SAWR-US)
"WOOD LIZARD"

INTERESTING FACTS:

The **Hylaeosaurus** was shaped like a barrel and had an armored plating on its body. It had spikes and spines sticking out of the armor which protected it from other dinosaurs. Because it had small teeth, it was a plant eater.

When It Lived

EARLY CRETACEOUS

Size
20 FEET

Weight
UNKNOWN

HYPSILOPHODON
(HIP-SIH-LOHF-O-DON)
"HIGH RIDGE TOOTH"

WHERE IT WAS FOUND
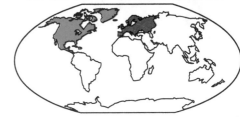
NORTH AMERICA AND EUROPE

INTERESTING FACTS:

The **Hypsilophodon** was a small plant eater that may have lived in herds. A short stiff tail helped balance its head and body as it ran swiftly from predators. It had no teeth at the front of its mouth but had chisel-like sharp teeth farther back.

When It Lived
EARLY CRETACEOUS
Size
6 FEET
Weight
130 POUNDS

IGUANODON
(IG-WAN-OH-DON)
"IGUANA TOOTH"

EUROPE, AFRICA, NORTH
AMERICA AND ASIA

INTERESTING FACTS:

In 1825, this creature became the second dinosaur to be named. It was named **Iguanodon** because its teeth resembled those of an iguana. Scientists could tell by the shape of its teeth, it was a plant eater. Its hands looked much like a human's, but the thumbs were short, sharp spikes. They were probably used as weapons and to hold on to branches to to help it munch leaves.

When it ran, it picked up its tail and leaned forward. When it stopped, it leaned back and rested on its tail.

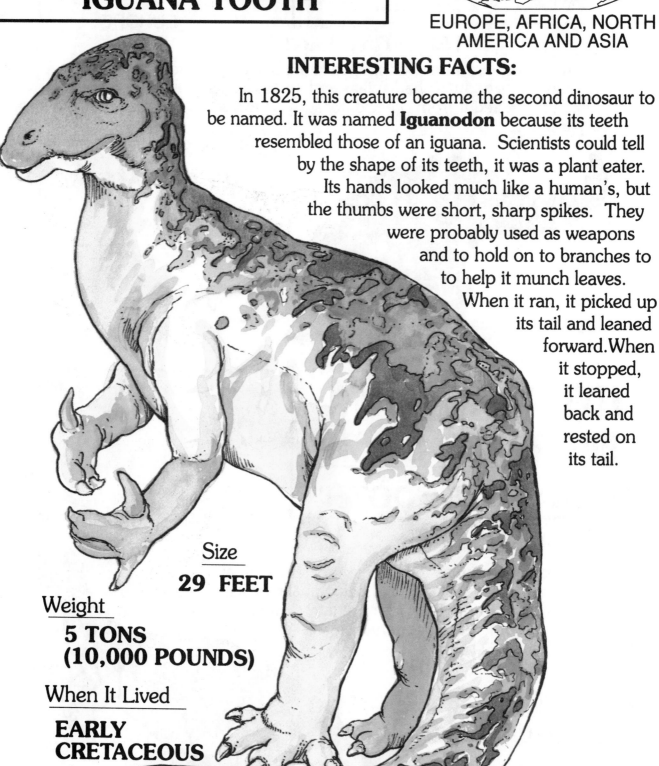

Size
29 FEET

Weight
5 TONS
(10,000 POUNDS)

When It Lived
EARLY
CRETACEOUS

INDOSUCHUS
(IN-DOH-SOOK-US)

"INDIAN CROCODILE"

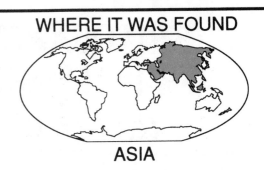
INTERESTING FACTS:

Despite its name, the **Indosuchus** had nothing to do with crocodiles. It was related to a Tyrannosaurus but its size was smaller. It had fewer and smaller teeth than its relative. This meat eater walked on its hind legs and had little use for its front legs.

When It Lived

LATE CRETACEOUS

Size

30 FEET

Weight

4 TONS (8,000 POUNDS)

KENTROSAURUS
(KEN-TRUH-SAWR-US)

"SPIKED LIZARD"

WHERE IT WAS FOUND

AFRICA

INTERESTING FACTS:

The **Kentrosaurus** had triangular-shaped plates on its neck and shoulders. Two rows of spikes ran along its back and tail. These spikes protected its body from attack. This plant-eating dinosaur walked on all fours.

Weight

1 TON (2,000 POUNDS)

Size

17 FEET

When It Lived

LATE JURASSIC

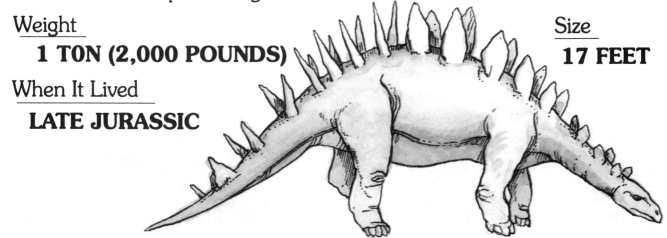

KRITOSAURUS
(KRIT-UH-SAWR-US)
"NOBLE LIZARD"

INTERESTING FACTS:

The **Kritosaurus** had a broad head with a hump on its nose. Webbed feet probably enabled it to swim. It walked through forests on its hind legs searching for plants to eat. Some scientists feel this may be a very close relative to the Hadrosaurus.

When It Lived

LATE CRETACEOUS

Size
30 FEET

Weight
3 TONS (6,000 POUNDS)

LAMBEOSAURUS
(LAM-BE-UH-SAWR-US)
"LAMBE'S LIZARD"

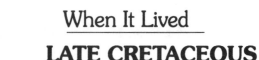

INTERESTING FACTS:

The **Lambeosaurus** was a duck-billed dinosaur with a broad beak. Plants were its main food. It had a large, unusually shaped crest on its head. It stood tall on its hind legs and had leathery skin. The **Lambeosaurus** had a very long tail.

Size
49 FEET

When It Lived

LATE CRETACEOUS

Weight

**2-5 TONS
(4,000-10,000 POUNDS)**

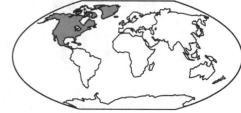

LESOTHOSAURUS
(LEH-SOTH-UH-SAWR-US)
"LESOTHO LIZARD"

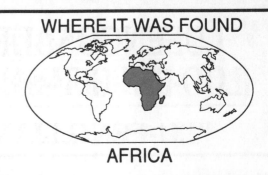

INTERESTING FACTS:

The **Lesothosaurus** was a small dinosaur about the size of a large dog. Small teeth lined the beak-like jaw in its little head. It probably ate plants when it was on all fours, but escaped danger by running swiftly on its two hind legs.

Size

3 FEET

Weight

40 POUNDS

When It Lived

LATE TRIASSIC/EARLY JURASSIC

LEXOVISAURUS
(LEX-OH-VUH-SAWR-US)
"LEXOVI LIZARD"

WHERE IT WAS FOUND

EUROPE

INTERESTING FACTS:

The **Lexovisaurus** had plates on its neck and back, and spines on its tail. Large spines stuck out sideways from its hips. This armor probably protected the animal from enemies. Plants made up its diet which it chewed with small teeth.

When It Lived

MIDDLE JURASSIC

Size

17 FEET

Weight

1 TON (2,000 POUNDS)

LUFENGOSAURUS
(LOO-FEN-GUH-SAWR-US)
"LU-FENG LIZARD

ASIA

Weight
1,800 POUNDS

Size
20 FEET

When It Lived
LATE TRIASSIC/ EARLY JURASSIC

INTERESTING FACTS:
The **Lufengosaurus** is one of the oldest dinosaurs found in China. It was probably able to walk upright on its powerful hind legs or on all fours. Its short, gapped-teeth had sharp edges. Scientists think its diet consisted of both plants and small animals.

MAIASAURA
(MAH-EE-AH-SAWR-US)
"GOOD MOTHER LIZARD"

WHERE IT WAS FOUND

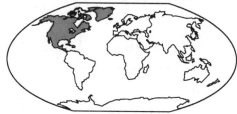

NORTH AMERICA

INTERESTING FACTS:

The **Maiasaura** was given its name "Good Mother Lizard" because skeletons were found near nests of eggs and with babies. Each nest was seven feet across and two feet deep. After hatching, the young dinosaurs probably stayed close to home. The mother may have cared for her young and probably brought them food.

When It Lived
LATE CRETACEOUS

Size
30 FEET

Weight
2 TONS (4,000 POUNDS)

MAMENCHISAURUS
(MAH-MEN-CHEE-SAWR-US)
"MAMENCHI LIZARD"

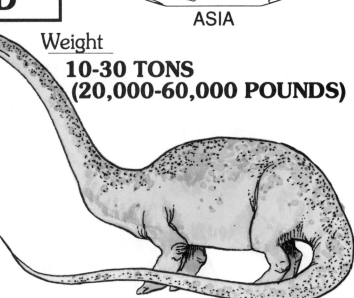

ASIA

When It Lived

LATE JURASSIC

Size

72 FEET

Weight

**10-30 TONS
(20,000-60,000 POUNDS)**

INTERESTING FACTS:

Scientists think that the **Mamenchisaurus** had the longest neck of any dinosaur ever found. It used its long neck to help it eat leaves from the top of trees. Four short legs had to work very hard to carry its huge heavy body.

MAMMUTHUS
(MAM-UHTH-US)
"WOOLY MAMMOTH"

WHERE IT WAS FOUND

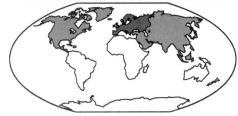

NORTH AMERICA, EUROPE
AND ASIA

INTERESTING FACTS:

The **Mammuthus** was one of the largest types of elephants that ever lived. Its entire body was covered with long thick hair. A three inch layer of fat beneath the hair helped keep it warm. It had two tusks in its lower jaw and a long trunk. Plants and grasses made up most of its diet.

When It Lived

ICE-AGE

Size

13 FEET HIGH

Weight

UNKNOWN

MASSOSPONDYLUS
(MASS-O-SPON-DIH-LUS)
"BULKY SPINY BONE"

WHERE IT WAS FOUND

AFRICA

When It Lived

LATE TRIASSIC/EARLY JURASSIC

Weight

1,200 POUNDS

Size

13 FEET

INTERESTING FACTS:

The **Massospondylus** was a very common early dinosaur. It had powerful hind legs and strong arms. Each hand had a huge thumb with a large, curved claw. This dinosaur may have eaten both meat and plants. Pebbles in its stomach probably helped grind up plants so they could be digested more easily.

MEGALOCERAS
(MEG-UH-LOW-SAIR-US)
"GIANT IRISH ELK"

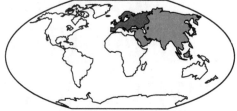

WHERE IT WAS FOUND

EUROPE AND ASIA

INTERESTING FACTS:

The **Megaloceras** was a giant deer. The male had antlers that could grow to ten feet across and weigh up to 150 pounds. It was a very fast runner that grazed in wooded areas for food.

When It Lived

ICE-AGE

Size

6 FEET TALL

Weight

UNKNOWN

MEGALOSAURUS
(MEG-UH-LO-SAWR-US)
"BIG LIZARD"

EUROPE

INTERESTING FACTS:

The **Megalosaurus** was a meat-eating dinosaur with very long claws on its toes and hands. It had huge fangs and knife-like teeth. It walked on its huge hind legs. The **Megalosaurus** was the first dinosaur discovered and named.

When It Lived

EARLY JURASSIC TO EARLY CRETACEOUS

Size

30 FEET

Weight

1 TON (2,000 POUNDS)

MEGATHERIUM
(MEG-UH-THEE-RIH-UHM)
"GIANT GROUND SLOTH or GIANT BEAST"

WHERE IT WAS FOUND

NORTH & SOUTH AMERICA

INTERESTING FACTS:

The **Megatherium** was a relative of today's tiny tree sloth only it was as big as an elephant. It had an enormous thick tail and long curling claws on its feet. Because of its claws it could not walk properly. It walked on the knuckles of its front feet and the sides of its back feet. These claws were probably used to dig up roots.

When It Lived

ICE-AGE

Size

20 FEET

Weight

UNKNOWN

MELANOROSAURUS
(MEL-AN-OR-UH-SAWR-US)

"BLACK MOUNTAIN LIZARD"

INTERESTING FACTS:

The **Melanorosaurus** was the largest early dinosaur. Few enemies were able to attack it because of its huge size. This plant eater walked on all fours and had very heavy legs like an elephant. Its neck and tail were extremely long and heavy bones supported its huge body.

When It Lived
LATE TRIASSIC/EARLY JURASSIC

Size
40 FEET

Weight
2 TONS
(4,000 POUNDS)

MICROCERATOPS
(MY-KRO-SAIR-UH-TOPS)

"TINY HORNED FACE"

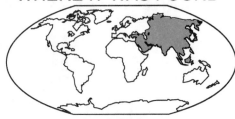

INTERESTING FACTS:

The **Microceratops** was one of the smallest dinosaurs ever found. This tiny plant eater had a horny beak that helped it dig for food. It searched for food on all fours but probably ran on its hind legs. Because of its small size, it was easy prey for larger dinosaurs.

When It Lived
LATE CRETACEOUS

Size
2 FEET

Weight
25 POUNDS

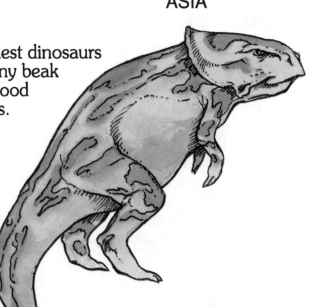

MICROVENATOR
(MY-KRO-VEN-AY-TOR)

"SMALL HUNTER"

NORTH AMERICA AND ASIA

INTERESTING FACTS:

The **Microvenator** was a lightweight turkey-size dinosaur. It had a small head and a long neck. There were three long fingers on each of its short arms. A long tail helped it keep its balance. This swift meat-eating dinosaur ran on its hind legs.

When It Lived
EARLY CRETACEOUS

Size
2 FEET

Weight
14 POUNDS

MONOCLONIUS
(MON-UH-CLO-NEE-US)

"SINGLE STEM"

WHERE IT WAS FOUND

NORTH AMERICA

INTERESTING FACTS:

The **Monoclonius** had a single, long horn growing on its nose and small bumps above its eyes. It had a short neck frill made of bone with two large holes in the frill. Scaly skin covered its body and its toes were hoofed. Its huge head stayed close to the ground where it grazed on plants.

When It Lived
LATE CRETACEOUS
Size
18 FEET

Weight
UNKNOWN

NODOSAURUS
(NO-DO-SAWR-US)

"KNOBBY LIZARD"

WHERE IT WAS FOUND

NORTH AMERICA

INTERESTING FACTS:

The **Nodosaurus** was covered with large and small armor-like plates. These plates made it difficult for other animals to attack this medium-sized dinosaur. Its tail dragged along the ground as it searched for soft plants to eat.

When It Lived

LATE CRETACEOUS

Size

18 FEET

Weight

**2-3 TONS
(4,000-6,000 POUNDS)**

ORNITHOLESTES
(OR-NITH-O-LESS-TEEZ)

"BIRD ROBBER"

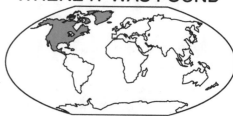

WHERE IT WAS FOUND

NORTH AMERICA

INTERESTING FACTS:

The **Ornitholestes** was a fast-running little dinosaur. It ran on its slim back legs and caught small lizards with its tiny clawed hands. Probably a scavenger, it ate the dead flesh of other dinosaurs it came upon while traveling swiftly through grassland areas.

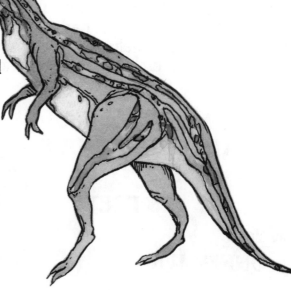

When It Lived

LATE JURASSIC

Size

6 FEET

Weight

30 POUNDS

ORNITHOMIMUS
(OR-NITH-UH-MY-MUS)
"BIRD IMITATOR"

When It Lived

LATE CRETACEOUS

Size

11 FEET

Weight

220 POUNDS

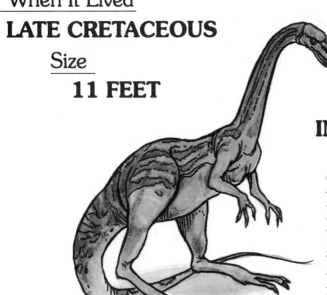

INTERESTING FACTS:

The **Ornithomimus** looked like an ostrich without feathers. It was lightly built, therefore, it could outrun any other animal. Its mouth contained no teeth so its beak probably broke up the insects, fruit and small animals which it ate. Because it had a large brain, it is believed to be one of the most intelligent dinosaurs.

OURANOSAURUS
(OUR-AHN-UH-SAWR-US)
"BRAVE MONITOR LIZARD"

INTERESTING FACTS:

The **Ouranosaurus** was a plant-eating dinosaur with very high spines running down its back and tail. These spines formed a kind of thin sail and may have acted as a solar panel to warm the animal. The **Ouranosaurus** could walk on all fours or its hind legs.

When It Lived

EARLY CRETACEOUS

Size

23 FEET

Weight

4 TONS (8,000 POUNDS)

OVIRAPTOR
(O-VEE-RAP-TOR)
"EGG THIEF"

INTERESTING FACTS:

The **Oviraptor** was a small dinosaur without teeth. It had a powerful beak that was able to crush bones and shells. This bird-like creature had large claws and long fingers it used to grasp its prey. It walked on two thin legs.

When It Lived

LATE CRETACEOUS

Size

6 FEET

Weight

60 POUNDS

PACHYCEPHALOSAURUS
(PAK-EE-SEF-UH-LO-SAWR-US)
"THICK-HEADED LIZARD"

WHERE IT WAS FOUND

NORTH AMERICA

INTERESTING FACTS:

The **Pachycephalosaurus** was a large dinosaur with a nine inch plate of bone covering its brain. It used its domed head as a weapon against enemies. This plant eater's tail was stiff and may have been used to help the dinosaur keep its balance.

When It Lived

LATE CRETACEOUS

Size

17 FEET

Weight

450 POUNDS

PACHYRHINOSAURUS
(PAK-EE-RYE-NO-SAWR-US)

"THICK-NOSED LIZARD"

INTERESTING FACTS:

The **Pachyrhinosaurus** was an unusual plant-eating horned dinosaur. Instead of a horn on its nose, it had a large plate of bone. In the middle of this plate was a volcano-shaped crater. Bony knobs grew above the eyes and one horn grew in the center of its neck frill.

When It Lived

LATE CRETACEOUS

Size

18 FEET

Weight

**1-2 TONS
(2,000-4,000 POUNDS)**

PANOPLOSAURUS
(PAN-OP-LUH-SAWR-US)

"ARMORED LIZARD"

INTERESTING FACTS:

The **Panoplosaurus** was a dinosaur with large armored plates protecting its head, neck, back and tail. Long spikes jutted out from its shoulders and sides. Surprisingly, this huge well-protected animal had small ridged teeth only good for eating plants.

When It Lived

LATE CRETACEOUS

Size

23 FEET

Weight

**3-4 TONS
(6,000-8,000 POUNDS)**

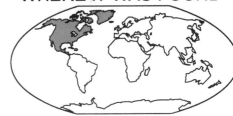

PARASAUROLOPHUS
(PAR-AH-SAWR-OL-UH-FUS)
"SIMILAR CRESTED LIZARD"

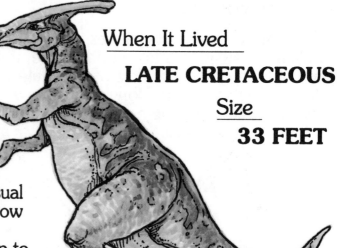

Weight

3 TONS (6,000 POUNDS)

When It Lived

LATE CRETACEOUS

Size

33 FEET

INTERESTING FACTS:

The **Parasaurolophus** was a very unusual duck-billed dinosaur. It had a tube-like hollow crest growing on the top of its head and extending outward. Breathing tubes ran up to the crest and into the mouth. This probably enabled it to make a sound like a trombone. Its diet consisted of pine needles and leaves.

PARROSAURUS
(PAR-UH-SAWR-US)
"PARR'S LIZARD"

INTERESTING FACTS:

The **Parrosaurus** had a very long neck it used to help it eat leaves off the top of trees. A long thick tail was used to help support its body if it reared up on its hind legs. Its brain was very small compared to the size of its body.

When It Lived

LATE CRETACEOUS

Size

40 FEET

Weight

30 TONS (60,000 POUNDS)

PENTACERATOPS
(PEN-TAH-SAIR-UH-TOPS)
"FIVE HORNED FACE"

When It Lived

LATE CRETACEOUS

INTERESTING FACTS:

The **Pentaceratops** had more horns on its head than any horned dinosaur. It had a short nose horn, one above each eyebrow, and a smaller one on each cheek. This plant-eating dinosaur's neck frill was very long and may have been used to scare off enemies.

Size

20 FEET

Weight

**2 TONS
(4,000 POUNDS)**

PINACOSAURUS
(PIN-AH-KUH-SAWR-US)
"BOARD LIZARD"

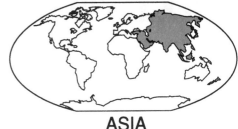
INTERESTING FACTS:

The **Pinacosaurus** had a hard armored back and tail. At the end of its tail was a big bony club. Sharp spikes stuck out along its back and sides. Its beak-like face and small teeth were well-suited for plant eating.

When It Lived

LATE CRETACEOUS

Size

18 FEET

Weight

2 TONS (4,000 POUNDS)

PLATEOSAURUS
(PLAY-TEE-UH-SAWR-US)
"FLAT REPTILE"

When It Lived

LATE TRIASSIC

Weight

UNKNOWN

INTERESTING FACTS:

The **Plateosaurus** was a large dinosaur with a very long neck and tail. It had many rows of triangular-shaped small teeth which helped it shred plants. It may have swallowed stones to help it grind up the plants in its stomach. The **Plateosaurus** may have roamed the earth in herds.

Size
**26 FEET LONG
15-20 FEET TALL WHEN
STANDING ON ITS HIND LEGS**

PROCOMPSOGNATHUS
(PRO-KOMP-SO-NAY-THUS)
"BEFORE ELEGANT JAW"

INTERESTING FACTS:

The **Procompsognathus** was a very small early dinosaur. It was less than 12 inches tall at the hips. Since it had hollow bones, it weighed very little. This tiny meat eater could run very swiftly and fed on insects and small animals.

Size
4 FEET

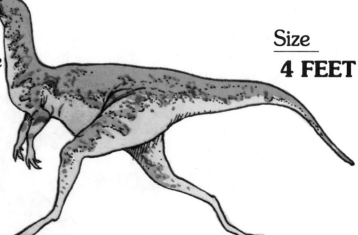

When It Lived

LATE TRIASSIC

Weight

15 POUNDS

PROSAUROLOPHUS
(PRO-SAWR-OL-UH-FUS)
"FIRST CRESTED LIZARD"

Weight
**14 TONS
(28,000 POUNDS)**

INTERESTING FACTS:

The **Prosaurolophus** was a duck-billed dinosaur that had a very small crest. This crest ran from its snout to the top of its head. It had small bony lumps above its eyes and a spike that pointed backwards. The adult **Prosaurolophus** laid its eggs in mounds of mud and may have looked after its young.

When It Lived

Size **26 FEET**

LATE CRETACEOUS

PROTOCERATOPS
(PRO-TOE-SER-A-TOPS)
"FIRST HORNED FACE"

INTERESTING FACTS:

The **Protoceratops** was one of the first horned dinosaurs. It was a small dinosaur that did not have a true horn but had a bony bump on its head above a large beak. This plant-eating dinosaur had teeth for chopping instead of chewing. The first dinosaur egg ever found was from a **Protoceratops**.

When It Lived

LATE CRETACEOUS

Size

**7 FEET LONG
30 INCHES HIGH**

Weight
**1.5 TONS
(3,000 POUNDS)**

PTERODACTYLUS
(TER-UH-DAK-TUH-LUS)
"WING FINGER"

INTERESTING FACTS:

The **Pterodactylus** was a tiny bird-like creature with wings but may not have had any feathers. It had a long neck, face and hands. Its leg muscles controlled the movement of its wings. Insects and small crustaceans were probably its main food.

When It Lived

LATE JURASSIC

Size

2 FEET

Weight

UNKNOWN

QUETZALCOATLUS
(KET-SOL-KO-AT-LUS)
"FEATHERED SERPENT GOD"

WHERE IT WAS FOUND

NORTH AMERICA

INTERESTING FACTS:

The **Quetzalcoatlus** was the largest flying creature that ever lived. It may have been able to fly for hours at a time. Its long, slender beak may have been used to spear fish or to find other food.

When It Lived

LATE CRETACEOUS

Size

40 FOOT WINGSPAN

Weight

150 POUNDS

SAICHANIA
(SYE-CHAY-NEE-AH)
"BEAUTIFUL ONE"

WHERE IT WAS FOUND

ASIA

INTERESTING FACTS:

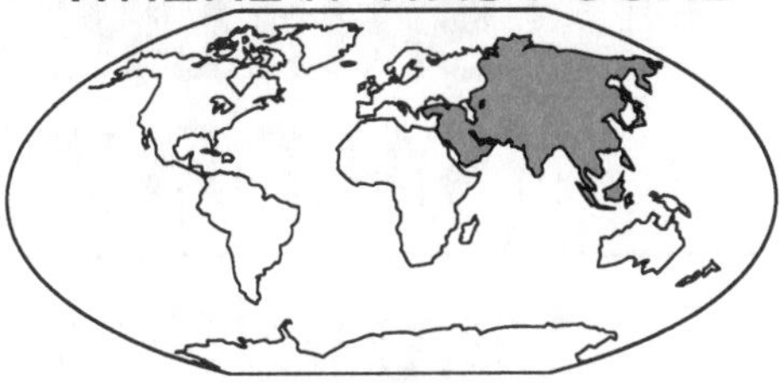

The **Saichania** was an armored dinosaur with its neck, back and stomach covered with bony plates and rows of spikes. Its tail had a bony club on the end of it. This club was probably used to attack flesh-eating dinosaurs. Many well-preserved skeletons of this plant eater have been found.

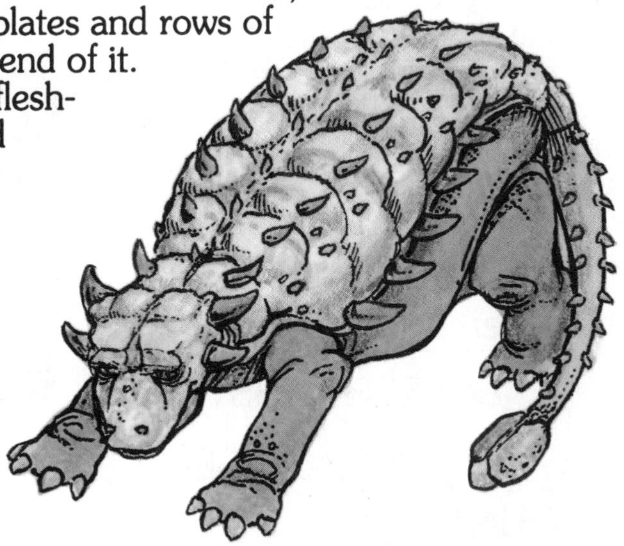

When It Lived

LATE CRETACEOUS

Size

23 FEET

Weight

3-5 TONS (6,000-10,000 POUNDS)

SALTASAURUS
(SALT-UH-SAWR-US)
"SALTA LIZARD"

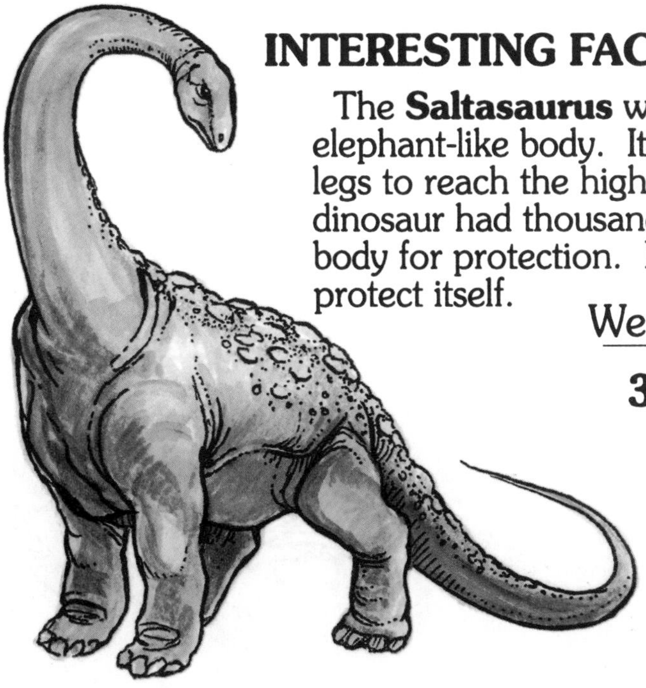

WHERE IT WAS FOUND

SOUTH AMERICA

INTERESTING FACTS:

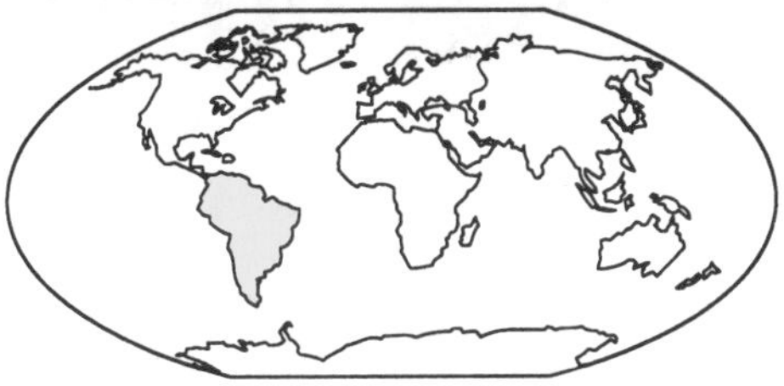

The **Saltasaurus** was a giant dinosaur with an elephant-like body. It could probably rear up on its hind legs to reach the highest branches of trees. This peaceful dinosaur had thousands of small armor plates all over its body for protection. It also used its long, thick tail to protect itself.

Weight

30 TONS (60,000 POUNDS)

When It Lived

LATE CRETACEOUS

Size

40 FEET

SALTOPUS
(SALT-O-PUS)
"LEAPING FOOT"

INTERESTING FACTS:

The **Saltopus** was a tiny, lightly built dinosaur which was able to run quickly from danger. It probably fed on insects and lizards. Its small hands had five fingers and could catch food. Standing only eight inches high, it was about the size of a cat.

When It Lived
LATE TRIASSIC

Weight	Size
2 POUNDS	**2 FEET**

SAUROLOPHUS
(SAWR-OL-O-FUS)
"CRESTED LIZARD"

WHERE IT WAS FOUND
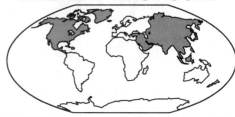
NORTH AMERICA AND ASIA

INTERESTING FACTS:

The **Saurolophus** was a duck-billed dinosaur with a horned crest that curved upward over the top of its head. Its long head was spoon-shaped. This plant eater had a strong muscular tail that helped it keep its balance when it stood on its hind legs.

Size
30 FEET

When It Lived
LATE CRETACEOUS

Weight
**1-2 TONS
(2,000-4,000 POUNDS)**

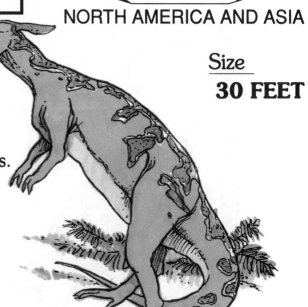

SAURORNITHOIDES
(SAWR-OR-NITH-OY-DEEZ)
"BIRD-LIKE LIZARD"

INTERESTING FACTS:

The **Saurornithoides** was one of the most intelligent of all the dinosaurs. It had a very large brain for its size. This meat eater had a long head with razor-sharp teeth. Keen eyesight and agility enabled it to be an excellent hunter.

When It Lived

LATE CRETACEOUS

Size

6 FEET

Weight

70 POUNDS

SCUTELLOSAURUS
(SCOO-TEL-OH-SAWR-US)
"LITTLE SHIELD LIZARD"

WHERE IT WAS FOUND

NORTH AMERICA

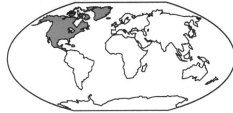

INTERESTING FACTS:

The **Scutellosaurus** was a small plant eater with triangular-shaped teeth in a single row. Tiny, bony knobs protected its body. A tail longer than its entire body may have been used to help keep its balance. It had long back legs and short front legs and could probably run swiftly.

When It Lived

LATE TRIASSIC/ EARLY JURASSIC

Weight

Size **50 POUNDS**

4 FEET

SEGISAURUS
(SEE-GIH-SAWR-US)
"SEGI LIZARD"

NORTH AMERICA

INTERESTING FACTS:

The **Segisaurus** was a small dinosaur about the size of a large rabbit or goose. It had slim hind legs that allowed it to run quickly from its enemies. It probably ate small lizards and insects.

When It Lived

EARLY JURASSIC

Size
3 FEET

Weight
20 POUNDS

SEISMOSAURUS
(SYE-MO-SAWR-US)
"EARTHSHAKER LIZARD"

WHERE IT WAS FOUND

NORTH AMERICA

INTERESTING FACTS:

The **Seismosaurus** may have been the longest dinosaur that ever roamed the earth. It was recently discovered in 1984 and scientists are still excavating the site where it was found. It walked on all fours and probably had a very long tail.

When It Lived
LATE JURASSIC

Size
120 FEET

Weight
80-100 TONS
(160,000-200,000 POUNDS)

SHANTUNGOSAURUS
(SHAN-TUNG-O-SAWR-US)

"SHANTUNG LIZARD"

INTERESTING FACTS:

The **Shantungosaurus** is the biggest duck-billed dinosaur ever discovered. Its head had a flat top and a flat beak. The front of this giant's mouth had no teeth so it chewed with its powerful jaw. It stored extra food in its cheeks to eat at a later time.

Size
39-49 FEET

Weight
**3-4 TONS
(6,000-
8,000 POUNDS)**

When It Lived
LATE CRETACEOUS

SMILODON
(SMY-LOH-DAHN)

"KNIFE TOOTH or SABERTOOTH CAT"

INTERESTING FACTS:

The **Smilodon** was a fierce meat-eating lion-like cat. It had a mouth full or razor-sharp teeth and a six inch long sharp fang curving down each side of its mouth. It could run swiftly only for a short distance so it lay in wait for its prey. Mastodons and elephants were favorite foods.

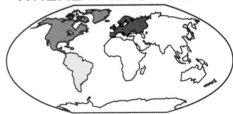

When It Lived
ICE AGE

Size
40 INCHES TALL

Weight
UNKNOWN

SPINOSAURUS
(SPY-NUH-SAWR-US)
"THORN LIZARD"

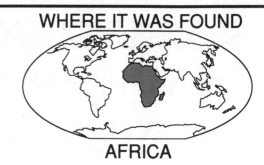

AFRICA

INTERESTING FACTS:

The giant **Spinosaurus** had six foot long spines on its back covered with skin. This sail-like structure may have regulated its body temperature. Knife-like straight teeth were used to tear into animal flesh.

When It Lived

LATE CRETACEOUS

Size

40 FEET

Weight

7 TONS (14,000 POUNDS)

STAURIKOSAURUS
(STOR-IK-UH-SAWR-US)
"LIZARD OF THE SOUTHERN CROSS"

WHERE IT WAS FOUND

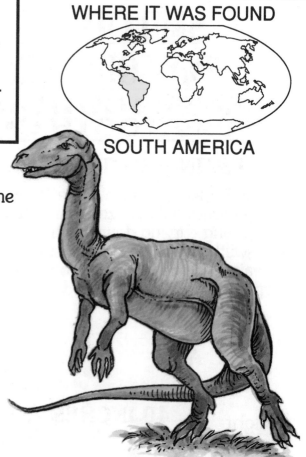

SOUTH AMERICA

INTERESTING FACTS:

Until recently, the **Staurikosaurus** was one of the oldest dinosaurs known. This meat-eating, small dinosaur probably had five-fingered hands and five-toed feet. It walked and ran very fast on two legs and had no known relatives.

When It Lived

MIDDLE TRIASSIC

Size

6 FEET 6 INCHES

Weight

65 POUNDS

STEGOSAURUS
(STEG-UH-SAWR-US)
"PLATED LIZARD"

INTERESTING FACTS:

The **Stegosaurus** is known for the big, bony plates on its neck and back. With its spiked tail, it defended itself against enemies. This scary-looking dinosaur had very small teeth and fed on plants and leaves.

When It Lived

LATE JURASSIC

Size

25 FEET

Weight

2 TONS (4,000 POUNDS)

STENONYCHOSAURUS
(STEN-ON-IK-UH-SAWR-US)
"NARROW-CLAWED LIZARD"

WHERE IT WAS FOUND

NORTH AMERICA

INTERESTING FACTS:

The **Stenonychosaurus** had a large brain and may have been one of the most intelligent dinosaurs. Its long, stiff tail helped it keep its balance and curved claws were used for grasping and holding its prey. Large eyes helped it to see clearly when it hunted.

When It Lived

LATE CRETACEOUS

Size

6 FEET

Weight

60-80 POUNDS

STYRACOSAURUS
(STY-RAK-UH-SAWR-US)
"SPIKED LIZARD"

INTERESTING FACTS:

The **Styracosaurus** was a lizard with a short frill. It had one horn on its nose and six huge spikes attached to the back of its neck frill. Its nose horn was used to dig up roots and other plants to eat and to protect itself. It was a scary-looking dinosaur.

Size
18 FEET

When It Lived
LATE CRETACEOUS

Weight
**3 TONS
(6,000 POUNDS)**

TARCHIA
(TAR-KEE-A)
"BRAINY"

INTERESTING FACTS:

The **Tarchia** was a plant eater with a triangular-shaped head covered with bony plates. Two bony horns stuck out from its skull and rows of spikes ran down its back and tail. A club at the end of its tail along with its armored body made it difficult to attack.

Size
28 FEET

When It Lived
LATE CRETACEOUS

Weight
**3-4 TONS
(6,000-8,000 POUNDS)**

THESCELOSAURUS
(THESS-UH-LO-SAWR-US)
"MARVELOUS LIZARD"

WHERE IT WAS FOUND

NORTH AMERICA

INTERESTING FACTS:

The **Thescelosaurus** may have been the last dinosaur on earth. Five fingers on each hand helped it claw for plant food and five fingers on each toe enable it to run very quickly. Rows of bony studs may have protected its back.

When It Lived

LATE CRETACEOUS

Size

12 FEET

Weight

UNKNOWN

TRICERATOPS
(TRY-SAIR-UH-TOPS)
"THREE-HORNED FACE"

WHERE IT WAS FOUND

NORTH AMERICA

INTERESTING FACTS:

This very large and heavy dinosaur had a smooth, solid frill. It had a small nose horn and two very large horns on its head. The **Triceratops** was slow-moving and used these horns to protect itself. Scientists have identified five different species of this dinosaur from the many skeletons discovered.

When It Lived

LATE CRETACEOUS

Size

25 FEET

Weight

6 TONS(12,000 POUNDS)

TYRANNOSAURUS REX
(TIE-RAN-UH-SAWR-US)
"TYRANT LIZARD"

INTERESTING FACTS:

The **Tyrannosaurus Rex** was probably the most powerful and biggest meat eater that ever lived. It stood on huge back legs, and its huge feet were equipped with very sharp claws. Since it was hard for the large beast to move quickly, it waited until a smaller animal was close by to capture it for food.

Its tremendous head was five feet long and its mouth was filled with huge dagger-like teeth. The **Tyrannosaurus Rex** was one of the most ferocious dinosaurs on earth.

When It Lived
LATE CRETACEOUS

Size
**40 FEET LONG
18 FEET HIGH**

Weight
7 TONS (14,000 POUNDS)

VELOCIRAPTOR
(VEL-LOSS-IH-RAP-TOR)

"SWIFT ROBBER"

INTERESTING FACTS:

The **Velociraptor** was a ferocious meat-eating dinosaur. It was small and agile and it could run quite fast. On the end of each of its three long fingers was a large claw it used to kill its prey. The **Velociraptor** was about the size of a man.

When It Lived

LATE CRETACEOUS

Size
6 FEET

Weight
UNKNOWN

VULCANODON
(VUL-CAN-O-DON)

"VOLCANO TOOTH"

WHERE IT WAS FOUND

AFRICA

INTERESTING FACTS:

The **Vulcanodon** was a large plant eater with small, sharp teeth. It had thick elephant-like legs and a very long, sloped neck and tail. No skull has ever been found, so scientists have to guess at what its head may have looked like.

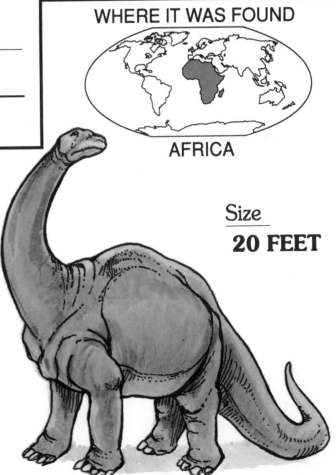

Size
20 FEET

When It Lived
EARLY JURASSIC

Weight
UNKNOWN

Fossils

Scientists learn about the history of the Earth by studying fossils. A fossil is the remains of an ancient animal or plant preserved in rock or some other material.

When the animal dies, it remains buried under mud or sand. The soft parts of the body decay leaving the bones, teeth or shells. It takes millions of years to change these hard animal parts and their surroundings into rock.

A leaf can leave an impression in coal or an insect may be preserved in hardened tree sap called amber. Fossils may also be found in ice or tar.

Footprints and skeletal remains are the most common form of dinosaur fossils. The picture below shows a dinosaur's footprints that were made in mud millions of years ago.

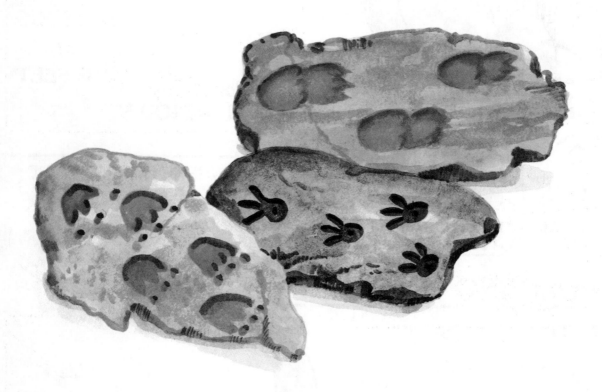

The skeletons of most dinosaurs have been found in sedimentary rock. Most sedimentary rock is formed in water. In time, the water dries up and the area that was under it becomes dry land. As erosion takes place, fossils embedded in the rock are exposed.

How A Fossil Is Formed

 A dinosaur drowns and sinks to the bottom of a river.

All of the flesh is eaten away or rots. Mud or sand covers up the bones.

 Mud and sand turn into rock after millions of years. The bottom of the river becomes exposed as the water subsides.

The rock is worn away by erosion and the dinosaur's skeletal remains can be seen.

Skin impressions and fossil eggs of dinosaurs have also helped scientists learn more about our ancient past. Fossil hunters search areas of the world where erosion has stripped away soil from rocks. Completely new groups of dinosaurs are still being discovered.

WHEN   THEY

PALEOZOIC ERA *AGE OF PLANTS, INSECTS,* *FISH AND AMPHIBIANS*		MESOZOIC *AGE OF*
PERMIAN **PERIOD** *began* *280 million years ago*	**TRIASSIC** **PERIOD** *began* *225 million years ago*	**JURASSIC** **PERIOD** *began* *190 million years ago*

	STAURIKOSAURUS	DILOPHOSAURUS
DIMETRODON		DIMORPHODON
		SEGISAURUS
		VULCANODON
	COELOPHYSIS	
	PLATEOSAURUS	CETIOSAURUS
	PROCOMPSOGNATHUS	DACENTRURUS
	SALTOPUS	DRYOSAURUS
		LEXOVISAURUS
		MEGALOSAURUS 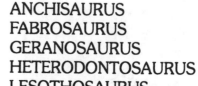

ANCHISAURUS
FABROSAURUS
GERANOSAURUS
HETERODONTOSAURUS
LESOTHOSAURUS
LUFENGOSAURUS
MASSOSPONDYLUS
MELANOROSAURUS
SCUTELLOSAURUS

ALLOSAURUS
APATOSAURUS
ARCHAEOPTERYX
BRACHIOSAURUS
CAMARASAURUS
CERATOSAURUS
COELURUS
COMPSOGNATHUS
DIPLODOCUS
ELAPHROSAURUS
KENTROSAURUS
MAMENCHISAURUS
ORNITHOLESTES
PTERODACTYLUS
SEISMOSAURUS
STEGOSAURUS

CAMPTO-

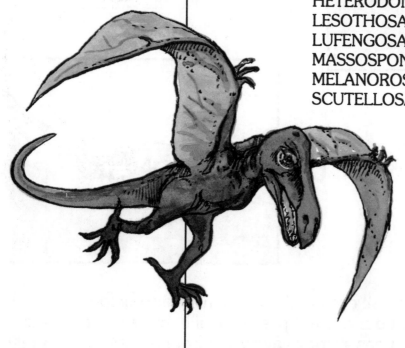
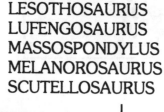

LIVED . . .

ERA *REPTILES*		CENOZOIC ERA *AGE OF MAMMALS*	
CRETACEOUS PERIOD *began* *135 million years ago*		**TERTIARY PERIOD** *began* *65 million years ago*	**QUARTERNARY PERIOD** *began* *2 million years ago*

(ICE AGE)

ALTISPINAX
DEINONYCHUS
HYLAEOSAURUS
HYPSILOPHODON
IGUANODON
MICROVENATOR
OURANOSAURUS

BACTROSAURUS

ACANTHOPHOLIS	PARASAUROLOPHUS
ALBERTOSAURUS	PARROSAURUS
ANATOSAURUS	PENTACERATOPS
ANCHICERATOPS	PINACOSAURUS
ANKYLOSAURUS	PROSAUROLOPHUS
AVIMIMUS	PROTOCERATOPS
BAGACERATOPS	QUETZALCOATLUS
BRACHYCERATOPS	SAICHANIA
CARNOTAURUS	SALTASAURUS
CENTROSAURUS	SAUROLOPHUS
CHASMOSAURUS	SAURORNITHOIDES
CORYTHOSAURUS	SHANTUNGOSAURUS
DASPLETOSAURUS	SPINOSAURUS
DROMAEOSAURUS	STENONYCHOSAURUS
DROMICEIOMIMUS	STYRACOSAURUS
EDMONTOSAURUS	TARCHIA
EOCERATOPS	THESCELOSAURUS
ERLIKOSAURUS	TRICERATOPS
EUOPLOCEPHALUS	TYRANNOSAURUS REX
HADROSAURUS	VELOCIRAPTOR
HOMALOCEPHALE	
INDOSUCHUS	
KRITOSAURUS	
LAMBEOSAURUS	
MAIASAURA	
MICROCERATOPS	
MONOCLONIUS	
NODOSAURUS	
ORNITHOMIMUS	
OVIRAPTOR	
PACHYCEPHALOSAURUS	
PACHYRHINOSAURUS	
PANOPLOSAURUS	

SAURUS

MAMMUTHUS

MEGALOCERAS

MEGATHERIUM

SMILODON

WHERE THEY LIVED...

Dinosaurs first appeared on Earth toward the end of the Triassic Period. They died out about 65 million years ago during the Cretaceous Period.

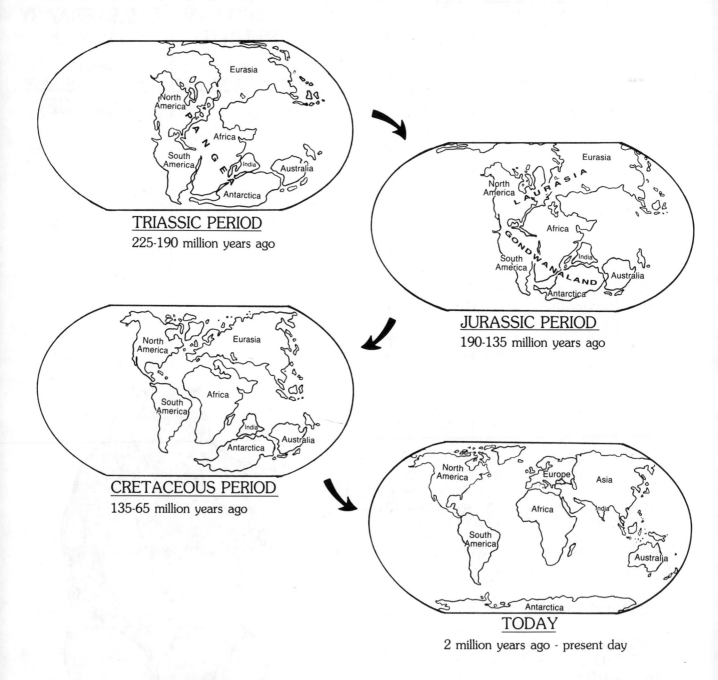

TRIASSIC PERIOD
225-190 million years ago

JURASSIC PERIOD
190-135 million years ago

CRETACEOUS PERIOD
135-65 million years ago

TODAY
2 million years ago - present day

Approximately 225 million years ago, all of the land masses on Earth were joined together. This one supercontinent was called Pangaea. It took millions of years for this huge land mass to break up and drift into the continents we know today. Millions of years from now the surface of the Earth will look different than it does today as the continental drift continues at a very slow pace.

Glossary

Amphibians - cold-blooded animals with backbones that are able to live on land and in the water

Biped - an animal that stands or walks on two hind legs

Birds - warm-blooded animals with backbones, feathers and wings

Camouflage - markings or color on an animal's skin or fur that makes it easy to hide in its environment

Carnivore - meat-eating animal

Cenozoic Era - 65 million years ago to the present including the Tertiary and Quarternary Periods

Climate - the weather of an area

Cold-blooded - not able to regulate body temperature

Crest - a growth on the top of an animal's head

Cretaceous Period - 135 to 65 million years ago

Dinosaurs - extinct animals that roamed the earth until 65 million years ago, means "terrible lizard"

Environment - the surroundings of an area

Erosion - wind, water, and other forces eating away at rock

Evolution - the gradual process and change by which animals and plants develop from earlier life

Extinct - no longer existing

Fangs - extra long, sharp teeth

Fossils - remains of an animal or plant preserved in rock

Frill - the flaring out of the back of the skull

Herbivore - plant-eating animal

Ice Age - period of time that began about 2 million years ago when the world became colder, winters became longer and ice covered much more of the earth's land than it does today

Insectivore - an insect eater

Invertebrate - animals without backbones

Jurassic Period - 190 to 135 million years ago

Mammals - warm-blooded animals with backbones, fur or hair that feed their young with milk from mammary glands

Mesozoic Period - 225 to 65 million years ago, the 160 million year time span during which dinosaurs and other prehistoric reptiles lived

Omnivore - animals that eat both plants and animals

Paleontology - the science of studying the past from geologic records and fossils

Paleozoic Era - 575 to 225 million years ago

Permian Period - 280 to 225 million years ago

Predators - animals that hunt and kill other animals

Prehistoric - time before written language existed

Prey - animals that are hunted and killed for food by other animals

Quadruped - an animal that stands or walks on four legs

Quarternary - 2 million years ago to present

Reptiles - cold-blooded animals with backbones, usually covered with scales or horny plates

Scavenger - an animal that eats the dead flesh of another animal it hasn't killed

Sedimentary rock - rock that has formed from mud or sand-mudstone, sandstone or limestone

Skeleton - all the bones of an animal that support the body

Talons - sharp claws

Tertiary Period - 65 to 2 million years ago

Triassic Period - 225 to 190 million years ago

Vertebrates - animals with backbone